Love After Death

D0879052

of related interest

Storymaking in Bereavement
Dragons Fight in the Meadow
Alida Gersie
ISBN 1 85302 176 8 pb
ISBN 1 85302 065 6 hb

The Forgotten Mourners
Guidelines for Working with
Bereaved Children
Sister Margaret Pennells and Susan C Smith
ISBN 1 85302 264 0

Grief in Children
A Handbook for Adults
Atle Dyregrov
ISBN 1 85301 113 X

Good Grief
Exploring Feelings, Loss and Death
with Under Elevens
Barbara Ward and associates
ISBN 1 85302 161 X

Good Grief
Exploring Feelings, Loss and Death
with Over Elevens and Adults
Barbara Ward and associates
ISBN 1 85302 162 8

Love After Death

Counselling in Bereavement

Mary Jones

Jessica Kingsley Publishers
London and Bristol, Pennsylvania

The right of Mary Jones to be identified as author of this work has been asserted by her in accordance with the Copyright, Designs and Patents Act 1988.

First published in the United Kingdom in 1995 by
Jessica Kingsley Publishers Ltd
116 Pentonville Road
London N1 9JB, England
and
1900 Frost Road, Suite 101
Bristol, PA 19007, U S A

Library of Congress Cataloging in Publication Data

A CIP catalogue record for this book is available from the Library of Congress

British Library Cataloguing in Publication Data

A CIP catalogue record for this book is available from the British Library

ISBN 1-85302-287-X

Printed and Bound in Great Britain by
Cromwell Press, Melksham, Wiltshire

With love to Georgina Evers, for her steadfast affection and understanding. You asked for 'plenty of stories' – and here they are.

Also in memory of Gianni, who couldn't quite wait for our birthday, March 1993

1

Bereavement

Is that a shocking first word to find in a book? I hope not. Will this be a sad and gloomy book, all about misery? Not necessarily.

Death and loss are universal. Everyone has someone who is special and close to them – after all, everyone has two parents. A person whose mother died in childbirth and whose father disappeared a week later has had a dramatic double loss. It may be different, but it can be just as painful a loss, in its own way, as that suffered by a woman whose husband has died after fifty-odd years of tranquil and amicable marriage.

Death, bereavement and the ensuing grief are as inevitable and natural as leaves falling in autumn. Nature has given us all a perfectly adequate in-built ability to deal with this. The vast majority of people work through their grief as healthily as most women work through their post-natal depression. But, as with some women, there may be a hiccough, some problem. Then

they need help to regain normal balance and control so that
they can get on with their lives.

We must all accept the inevitability and universality of death.
In our daily routine, personal or professional, we shall undoub-
tedly meet someone – a friend, a client, perhaps a member of
our family, who has suffered a major bereavement. Surely it can
only be helpful to understand something of what is happening
to them.

Psychiatrists refer to bereavement as 'the loss of a significant
loved one'. While it may not be possible to better this phrase
for accuracy, it is also somewhat cumbersome. For the sake of
simplicity only I shall refer to 'a widow'. But it cannot be
stressed too strongly that the effect of a major bereavement is
the same for everyone, regardless of what the relationship to
the dead person has been.

I have several qualifications for writing this book. First, I am
a widow. No one can read this with the thought at the back of
their head that 'Oh, well! It's all right for her! *She* doesn't know
what it's like' or 'It takes a widow to understand a widow!'

I do.

It is, in fact, not necessary to be a widow to understand the
process of grief. There is a massive bibliography in the recom-
mended reading list for any counsellors' training course. Bereavement has been studied, and studied – and studied. In the
prickly arrogance of my own widowhood, I subjected these
studies to the acid test of my own experience and was somewhat
irritated to find that I could not fault them.

But there is a gap between the clinical study and the raw
emotions of the newly bereaved. Because I have been on both
sides of the fence I can perhaps bridge the gap and explain
some of the difficulties.

There is, inevitably, much pain and confusion at the death of someone we have loved deeply. I see no reason at all why this should be made worse by fears born of ignorance. Death happens all the time, but few of us talk about it and its effect. That is why I have chosen to write this book, and I hope that I can articulate many of the feelings common to all widows.

For some years I have worked as a bereavement counsellor. I realise that, while the pain of bereavement is inevitable, some people need help and can be helped very successfully to become fully-functioning people again. Because of my experience, I can see bereavement now with some detachment.

The very statement that I am a counsellor may provoke some feelings of impatience and irritation. 'Counsellors! New-fangled, modern rubbish! There seem to be counsellors for everything under the sun today!', and following on the heels of these comments, 'When *my* husband died I just had to get on with things, grit my teeth, show some backbone. I endured. I saw it through on my own. I managed!'

Were such comments to be made to my face, it might come as a surprise to find that I should entirely agree with them. Very many people do resolve their grief perfectly satisfactorily. There are others who seem to do so; they go back to work, get on with bringing up the family, but they are not people who look happy. Often they seem prematurely aged, people over whom neighbours shake their heads and say, 'Never really got over Tom's death, but then, you never do really recover, do you?'

How true this is rather depends on what is the expectation. To get over someone's death, and to forget them are rather different things. To be a human being, capable of enjoying life on your own is difficult, but it is also perfectly possible.

❦ ❦ ❦ ❦ ❦ ❦ ❦ ❦ ❦ ❦

The trouble with the death of a significant loved one is that it is a unique experience. We have no frame-work, nothing previously learned, nothing to fall back on to help us with the unexpected problems.

After all, as we mature, we learn how to deal with a good many difficult situations and one experience teaches us how to cope when a similar one occurs later on. The first time we are in a position of danger we feel shock: for example in a car accident, we experience shock and all its alarming and frightening symptoms. The next time we feel shock the effects still occur, but a small voice at the back of the mind says, 'Oh, yes, I remember. I felt this last time. I know what happens'. This knowledge does not stop 'the happening' but it does take away the fear of the unknown.

For each woman the birth of a first child is a highly emotional experience. She may expect to have further children and with the birth of the next child she will, to some extent, be prepared for the experience. Subsequent births can never bring the alarm of the unknown.

Death, that other great hinge and landmark in life is different. There is no preparation for what we shall feel.

₪ ₪ ₪ ₪ ₪ ₪ ₪ ₪ ₪

The newly bereaved can never realise what a threat they present to many of those people to whom they most naturally turn for comfort. The woman's pain may embarrass her friends and family. Her very widowhood is a threat.

Each couple may deny it, may well not wish to recognise the reality, but the stark fact is that the new widow is a living proof that they themselves have a fifty–fifty chance of being in *her* situation. The non-bereaved find this frightening. There is a sense of alienation and in her widowhood the widow is slightly menacing. She knows what IT is like. She has come back, like Lazarus come back from the dead, and ordinary people know nothing of the fairy-tale monsters she has encountered in the underworld journey of her grief – nor do they wish to do so.

In their painful unhappiness, many widows simply grit their teeth, and their expectation is that they must just endure. In some ways they are right, because they alone can work through their grief. There are no short cuts and no one can take their pain away. But there is no reason at all why this pain, the missing, the loss, should be accompanied by panic and fear. Not one of us *has* to feel isolated. Shared knowledge that other people have experienced the same disturbing emotions can surely only be comforting and can help to reduce the level of agitation.

There are, for example, two symptoms thrown up by early grief that are so common that they might be considered universal. They are transient, and are hardly ever mentioned, but they are both highly inconvenient and extremely bewildering.

One is short-term memory loss, which can mean that a widow will have forgotten a telephone message and conversation by the time she has walked back from the hall to her sitting-room. New widows should walk round with a pen and note pad in their pocket all the time. Perhaps the new widow is going shopping and by the time she has walked across the road she cannot remember what she was going to buy. She is haunted by a fear that she will forget her keys. It is always awkward to be locked out of your own house but now there is no husband at home to answer her knock on the door.

There is, too, the feeling of exhaustion. It is quite usual for a new widow to be unable to get up from her chair and walk the few steps to the kettle to make a cup of tea. It may be some ten or fifteen minutes before she can bring herself to do so. She is not being lazy. She is not going out of her mind. She is not becoming paralysed. She is experiencing grief.

In those early days after a death there is a great need for sensitive, practical help – and that is something almost anyone can give.

Kind friends and neighbours say, 'Do let me know if there is anything I can do, you've only to ask' and feel pleased with themselves for offering help. It becomes quite another matter if a widow should say, 'Well, as a matter of fact there is...'

She may have come from a background where there was a touchy pride, 'We keep ourselves to ourselves'. Perhaps she and her husband had a professional and social role where people usually turned to *them* for help – maybe the deceased had been a vicar, a doctor or a headmaster. Now the roles are reversed and it is she who is the supplicant, and she finds this humiliating and uncomfortable.

After a death, those left behind have to adapt to new roles and learn different skills, take on new responsibilities. This is never easy and is particularly hard because it comes at a time when the widow feels least like doing anything at all.

The need for clean clothes is a problem likely to crop up quite quickly. A widower may never have been to a launderette and feels very shy. He doesn't know quite what to do, where to put the soap, and is afraid that the place will be populated entirely by women who will snigger about him.

The widower may never have ironed in his life before, and may find that while he can manage handkerchiefs and pillow cases, he has a very poor hand when it comes to sheets and shirts. He now recognises that throughout their married life his wife dealt with these, and with an easy competence – and he also feels sad and guilty that he had never once considered or acknowledged her skill.

Today most young husbands can change the baby's nappy just as well as their wives and, before marriage, in shared flats, routinely cooked and shopped and cleaned. Fifty years ago, the man who has now become a widower probably lived at home before marriage. He has never had to consider domestic problems before – and resents them. They all seem practical pinpricks, and they are all telling him how much he is missing his wife.

In the early days of grief, people cannot concentrate easily. Perhaps a wife has never been very good at filling in forms, having always left 'that sort of thing' to her husband. Now, she looks at them but they are meaningless to her, they make no sense. But she *has* to deal with DHSS forms so that she can claim her pension, and yet she cannot understand them. Very new widows – and widowers – need help in small, practical ways.

The tiredness and the memory loss are two symptoms. They may seem trivial, but while they last they present very real problems. It is in these areas where help is so often needed. The widow feels bewildered, because she feels unlike her normal self. In a time of great upheaval she is looking for some security and familiarity, and she becomes frightened easily because she, herself, is suddenly so different.

There are other things. She may often find that she is grinding her teeth involuntarily, and hopes she does not do this in public. She is slightly afraid of going outdoors, of being out in the open. The sky seems very high and white and almost threatening. She finds crossing a busy road hazardous because she has lost confidence in her ability to gauge the speed of the traffic.

At a time of new bereavement a woman may well suffer from a total loss of confidence. Most of us suffer from this occasionally, and very unpleasant it is, too. Because it is so common, and usually so transitory, there is a tendency to shrug it off and ignore it. But for a woman who has hitherto been extremely capable and independent, the effect is very unsettling. We probably know her; she is of a type; an efficient and competent woman. She has well-defined views on all manner of subjects, views which she expresses frequently. She may have been married to a successful man. She has brought up a family, and the children are now establishing themselves in the world. She has run a home, smoothly, and taken part in all manner of local activities.

One day, after her husband's death, she is driving along a dual carriageway from a shopping trip to the local supermarket, and a red light flashes up on the dashboard. A red light! A warning light! She is panic-stricken. She does not know what it is indicating. She wonders, wildly, if the car is about to explode. She is not sure if the car manual is in the glove compartment, and anyway she cannot stop on a busy road and read a book. She finds it difficult to concentrate and is by no means certain that she could understand the directions. The car, its maintenance, is something her husband always dealt with. She knows about petrol, checking the oil and, stiffly, she can do the tyre pressures.

The red light keeps on and on. Is it worse if the light is on constantly or if it is flickering? She puts her foot on the accelerator, longing only for the safety of home and the locked front door, praying the car is not about to explode.

We need to be confident before we can be amusing, telephone a friend, make a good story, share the fright: 'You'll never guess what an idiot I made of myself the other day. There was this sudden light in the car...'

None of us likes to appear a fool. If you have frightened yourself badly, you are more likely to wrap up the hurt secretly inside yourself.

Never think bereavement is simple.

These symptoms rarely last very long – perhaps only a few weeks. And they pass, quite naturally. But they are very trying at the time, especially when there are so many other, bigger problems.

Widowhood is rather more than 'the loss of a significant loved one'. What friends and family may not recognise – and what, indeed, she herself may hardly realise fully – is that she has lost herself. Among other things, she has lost her previous status in society.

As an extreme example, on the death of her husband, a Queen instantly becomes a 'Queen Mother'. Her son succeeds to the throne, her daughter-in-law becomes The Queen. Every 'ordinary' widow, when filling in forms, has to tick a new box when asked Married, Divorced, Single or Widow. Every time she has to do this she may feel a prick of sorrow and recognise a new classification.

This, of course, is only an outward manifestation of what is happening internally. For perhaps many years, she has felt not so much an individual but as part of another person and part of that relationship called marriage which they created between them. The wife may have submerged herself – and perhaps very willingly – in her husband and her children. On her husband's death, she has to confront herself. She cannot go back to being the person she once was, when she was a young woman. She now has to take on a new role, a new status, and she does not know how to play the part.

Grieving is very hard work: perhaps the widow and her husband colluded in the way they shared different responsibilities within the marriage.

Perhaps the husband had left the social side of their life to his wife. It was she who bought, wrote and sent the Christmas cards, kept in touch with friends they had met on holiday, contacted his ancient Auntie Flo, arranged the family parties and the reunion dinners with friends. Perhaps the wife always said, 'Oh, I'm hopeless about money, I leave all that to Bill', because she did not like dealing with such things as mortgages, Income Tax forms, pensions plans and the like. All her married life she has been able to wriggle out of facing these issues, but as a widow she has to confront them. Her reluctance to do so may be as strong as ever, but now there is no choice.

Her widowhood is not made the easier because other major events in her life were her own decisions. She, in accepting her husband's proposal, decided to get married. She probably planned her children. But death did not consult her. It happened. Something just as fundamental as those other events occurred without her permission, and she was catapulted into a strange land, wandering in a place where all the sign posts are blank.

It is hardly surprising, then, she frequently feels terrified, outraged and extremely angry. One could hardly expect her to feel otherwise. But these are not feelings that she will be able to share very readily.

It may be that you are seeing a widow in a counselling situation, or that you are simply being a kindly and caring person; perhaps you have asked the new widow – as a friend or neighbour – to come and have tea.

Watching her, you will see that she doesn't look very well, that she is inclined to be tearful. This is only to be expected. She seems lonely, rather lost and confused. These are feelings you would also expect.

But your 'widow' may also be bitter, snappy and so short-tempered that afterwards you comment to a mutual friend, 'She was positively rude! It'll be a long time before *I* ask her round again, I can tell you! I just don't know what's got into her!'

And that is the whole point. You don't know what has got into her. How much more terrifying for her, because she doesn't know what has 'got into her', either. There are all kinds of uncontrollable and alien feelings inside her, sweeping back and forth like invading barbarian hordes.

She may be silently screaming with rage at her husband. 'How dare you die and give me so much pain! You always said you loved me, and now you've abandoned me. You've left me to cope with all these horrid problems – the undertaker, the bank manager, and the Registrar. You always dealt with things like that, and I just can't manage. You should be here, to take care of me. There was that obscene telephone call the other night, and that funny man from upstairs... he quite scares me...'

The fact that part of her knows perfectly well that her late husband didn't *want* to die, didn't *ask* to develop cancer or have that heart attack, only adds to her confusion.

Rational knowledge does not take away her feelings, and the confusion is terrifying. She wonders if she is going mad. All these conflicting thoughts, jostling about together like a panic-stricken football crowd trying to escape through one small turnstile – make her hostility and prickliness entirely explicable.

I would, with diffidence, offer a theory that this anger – uncomfortable and socially damaging as it may be – has some use. I cannot believe that an emotion which presents almost universally after a recent death has been put there by nature for no purpose.

Life always has dangers, real or imagined. When there is an element of threat from the jungle outside, a married couple closes ranks, and the partners support, reassure and comfort each other. A widow has to face problems alone. It seems possible that the anger activates and serves as her essential survival-kit to defend herself, and to protect herself. Anger only becomes dangerous if it turns inward. Because the grief from a major bereavement is such a time of emotional vulnerability, anger can lead to depression, alcoholism and even suicide.

As doctors know, it is quite common for widows to present with symptoms of the disease which killed their husbands. It is as if, by developing these very symptoms, they can still be close to that husband, know exactly what he felt like, at the last. It is as if, in a very convoluted way, they wish to practise a kind of sympathetic magic.

I remember a young girl whose fiancé was driving to meet her one evening when he was killed in a car crash. Helga said, 'I had to go, I had to see the car. I found out from the police the name of the garage where the wreck had been taken. I went there, and I lied. I pretended I was from the insurance company. I had to sit in the car. I had to be behind the driving wheel, to see what Johnny saw at that last moment. I held the steering wheel as he would have held it. I looked at the dials on the dashboard that he had looked at. I had to do it. I wondered just what he'd felt like, although the police said that death was almost instantaneous. I felt close to him. It was lovely!'

Don't expect the newly bereaved to be very rational – they won't be!

❀ ❀ ❀ ❀ ❀ ❀ ❀ ❀ ❀ ❀

However, over a cup of tea, as she sniffs into her hanky, a widow is extremely unlikely to talk about such matters. After all, she herself may hardly be aware of them. And there may be other feelings that she won't talk about readily, either, because she is ashamed of them.

Wives, the world over, know that husbands are not always ideal creatures (and nor, perhaps, are wives). Your widow may, quite simply, find herself sighing with relief.

If his illness had been long – with a heavy burden of nursing at home, or tiring and complicated hospital visiting with a long daily journey – the relief at the death will, to a large extent, be practical and physical. If this is commented on, the widow may well hear such remarks with rather mixed feelings; it is surprising how commonly they are made.

We must admit that, however deeply we love, we love imperfectly. The ensuing guilt and remorse after death are painful and difficult: 'If only I hadn't lost my temper that day...': 'Why did I never understand that *that* meant so much to him?' She remembers being selfish and impatient. She remembers times when she brushed his feelings to one side. Then there are all the times she meant to say 'Sorry' and somehow never did – and now it is too late.

Similarly, there will have been times, in a long relationship, when *she* was hurt, even if only by some careless indifference or rejection. She has never received acknowledgement for this and so there is still some old resentment; now matters can never be put right. She, who never dared to say, 'Don't talk to me like that!' now acknowledges that she was slightly afraid of him. Perhaps there was an infidelity. The matter was glossed over, the marriage survived – but the fact of that affair can never be totally forgotten.

These sorts of feelings are known as unfinished business, and unfinished business needs particular tender, loving care before the hurts can be admitted, talked about and so resolved healthily. Until this is done, the memories cause festering problems, as though they were long black emotional splinters embedded in the heart. It is always very difficult to come to terms with ambivalence.

2

One person with such problems was... well, I think of her as Gloria.

I saw her for the first time about ten months after her husband's death. Although it had been a complete and devastating shock to Gloria, apparently they had both been warned about Tom's heart condition over a year before. Gloria had 'blocked out' the specialist's prognosis and was in a panic when Tom was rushed to hospital one midnight.

She had behaved impeccably. She had visited during all the permitted hours. The consultant and the sister both said after two days that, although Tom was very ill, he was improving, and there was no immediate danger. When they chivvied Gloria off at the end of visiting hours one evening, she realised she had no food at home, so she went to a local restaurant and stood herself a good meal. When she got home at midnight there was a telephone message to say that Tom had had a sudden relapse and that she should come at once. Unfortunately, by the time she got a taxi and reached the hospital, he had died.

That was tragic and most painful. But what I could not understand was her immense sense of guilt.

'I should have stayed,' she kept saying. 'I should have insisted. There I was, eating curry – and all the while he was dying!'

Gloria worked herself up into a paroxysm not so much of crying but of howling, and these tears did nothing to release her emotions. They had been married, as she told me at our first meeting, for thirty-five and a quarter years. Their only daughter was married, happy and busy with four children. There was no doubt that Gloria loved her Tom. It had been a deep relationship and yet she seemed to be refusing to let herself be comforted.

She showed me the family photographs and I 'met' Tom, laughing in the sun, with a decided twinkle in his eye. I thought he might have been a bit of a rogue, but he would have been great fun at a party.

One day, Gloria suddenly said, 'Of course, he could be very difficult. He wasn't an easy man. Our marriage wasn't always very smooth, let me tell you!' 'Marriages seldom are,' I commented. She paused, for a long time. 'There was someone else, for me. Just once. Didn't mean anything, you know.' I waited. Then, in flushed haste, she said, 'Well, actually, there were two... but it was a long time ago.'

I wondered about Tom. The photos had shown them on various holidays. In each one, he had his arm round another woman's waist. But I had seen Gloria's pain as well as her protestation of love, and I knew: 'You loved him best...'

When she cried, her tears hurt her, but they were true and healing.

❧ ❧ ❧ ❧ ❧ ❧ ❧ ❧ ❧ ❧

Bereavement is a major emotional earthquake. All familiar ground is thrown into turmoil. Old, old memories surge back vividly from ten, twenty, even forty years past. Total recall can be very uncomfortable and new widows are extremely sensitive. But most people learn to forgive, and in doing so, forgive themselves.

A widow may find she is often – and with shame and guilt – thinking, 'Thank goodness, I don't have to put up with his untidiness any longer...' or 'his domineering ways' or 'his meanness'. Perhaps her late husband had a violent temper.

She may have, occasionally, had to put up with physical abuse, even cruelty. Here we are not talking about 'battered wives' which is quite another question. But there are other forms of 'domestic violence' which surface either because of the inherent tensions in a close relationship or simply because a spouse happens to be the nearest person to hand on whom to vent frustration.

The wife may have had to endure oral abuse. Perhaps her husband had constantly belittled her, and her habitual lack of confidence makes it extremely difficult for her to cope with the problems of widowhood. Yet, in the teeth of all the apparent evidence to the contrary, she felt, and still feels, 'He didn't really mean it'. She forgives him because she loves him.

A woman may have had her nose broken by her husband and yet celebrate their ruby wedding. During the intervening thirty-eight years, she may often have wondered why she stood it and, when her husband dies, peacefully and in his sleep, she will have to confront that question, yet again.

But it is not easy. None of us find it acceptable to be glad that someone has died. Guilt and shame cause a widow conflict and confusion, all muddled in with the fact that she is genuinely missing her husband. A woman may never talk about these feelings; she is ashamed of them and she pushes them down inside herself, but they will all still be there, festering away.

She might make an oblique reference to them – just a few words. Perhaps her married daughter has come over to spend a day, to help sort out the clothes, and her mother sighs: 'He did have such a temper, didn't he? I used to worry about you children...'

The daughter, after all, remembers that temper herself, and can respond: 'We understood. We didn't really mind. He'd shout and stamp about and make a lot of noise, but we knew it didn't really mean anything. We knew he loved us and we always knew you loved him.'

But not everyone can come to terms with such matters so readily. Although she was an extreme case, I think of Agnes...

She was in her late sixties when I saw her, and she had been married for forty-four years. She had three children, all married, and her flat was festooned with photographs of grandchildren. Her husband had died about two years before. Although it had been rather sudden, it cannot have been unexpected because he had been attending our local hospital for a heart condition.

He had been in the building trade all his life. He was a master plasterer. Plasterers are always in demand and he had always been in work. He was a high wage-earner. He had made all the major and practical decisions in the family. As Agnes put it to me, 'Bills? What are bills? I've never paid a bill in my married life! I wouldn't know what a bill was if it came and looked me in the face!'

So, he had been a good provider and a protector. But, as Agnes talked to me, she told me that it had been his habit all their married life to go down to the local Working Men's Club on Friday and Saturday nights. There, he would get a skinful of whisky and when he was 'with drink taken' he would come home and he would beat her. Now, if someone beats you, they hurt you and if you are hurt, you are afraid. At some stage the situation must have been pretty serious, because she mentioned the involvement of the Social Services.

With his death, Agnes had lost a major protector and provider. But she had also lost a violent bully and she was struggling to come to terms with two very conflicting sets of emotions.

Unhappily, they were too strong for her, or she did not have the inner resources to confront them. She would not see me again and when I consulted her then social worker at the hospital, who had made the referral, she said they had found the same pattern. We both had made a second appointment, stood on the doorstep and seen the net curtain twitch. But for neither of us would Agnes open the door again.

Often there is a problem arising in grief from an estrange-ment. There has been a quarrel… perhaps an elder sister who had always felt the younger was the favoured one. After their mother's death, somehow it was the younger who had the greater share of the jewellery, and the two women fought most bitterly. Perhaps the younger died first, and the elder one had no opportunity to say sorry, to say a proper good-bye. There had been a bitterness, preventing the young cousins ever getting to know each other, a long division in the family. And with death, it is too late…

This problem is thrown up in its most acute form where there is an element of the unexpected; death by an accident, perhaps, and therefore an inherent feeling of violence. A woman died when a blood vessel ruptured in her brain and afterwards her daughter said, 'I have the feeling she was hacked down by machetes'.

The feeling that you have not said a proper goodbye is very painful.

Gilly was very young – under thirty. She had a daughter of seven and a son of four. About three years before, her Bill had become a heroin addict, and had died a year later.

Gilly had fought with all the desperate and painful futility with which anyone fights their partner's addiction. One morning, Bill announced he was going off to get his fix. She tried to stop him, but he knocked her away from the door. As he clattered up the steps, she screamed after him, 'If you get any more of that muck, I hope it fucking kills you!'

And it did. That night.

They were the last words she ever spoke to her husband, and she loved him very deeply. It does not take much imagination to realise Gilly had some major problems. Not only was it important for her, as a person, to come to terms with her guilt and anger and so resolve her grief – she had a life expectancy of some sixty years. She was, also, the mother of two very young children – and an excellent mother she was, too; they were a credit to her.

She was not so much concerned about her son – he had only been a toddler when Bill died – as about Maria. I asked her what she had told the children. 'I thought I'd better tell them the truth, so they won't be ashamed.' 'That must have been very hard.' Gilly ran her hand over her cropped blond hair. 'Yeah, in a way. I just said some bad men had given Dad stuff that didn't agree with him, and then he couldn't stop and it killed him. But that he was a good man, and a good Dad and that he'd loved his children.' 'And you?' 'Yes, and me. He loved us all. It was just that muck that got in the way.'

Gilly was so brave and truthful. Time and again, this is what comes up – how honest and courageous people are. We managed to talk through her feelings – and Gilly taught me about crying.

One day, she found her really deep pain. She sat doubled up on the sofa as if she had a bad period pain, and she started to cry. She cried and cried; howled and moaned, and went on crying. I became alarmed, and various possibilities occurred to me, born from pulp novels. Should I slap her face? Throw a glass of water over her? I didn't know the layout of the flat or where the kitchen was. And I was afraid to leave her on her own. She huddled herself into the corner of the sofa, so I just sat and held her hand. That proved the best thing to do, because in the end she stopped.

People have a natural switch-off mechanism. And, after all, she was crying from pain and not from hysteria. Eventually, she wiped her eyes, lifted a beautiful smooth face to me and said, 'Golly, I feel simply wonderful!' Rather wryly I thought to myself, 'Lucky you!'

Naturally, the stories of Agnes and Gilly are extreme cases and they are cited to make a point. They show that grief is not quite as placid and straightforward as it might first appear. People don't always just cry for a little while and get over it in a few weeks.

One of the complications about a bereavement is that the presenting loss may well have triggered off another, old and unresolved grief. People say, 'I feel much more upset than I had expected I would'. Very often, for instance, in their counselling, a client will casually mention, 'My Gran died when I was eleven. Ever such a lovely lady, she was. We were very close, you know. And when she died, I could never talk about it…'

Perhaps, here, I might insert a word of caution. When talking – and listening – to a widow be careful about 'comparing notes'. It is a great temptation to do so; you feel all lovely and close, cosy and intimate – but be careful what you say. It is possible some old grief of our own may have come up and, quite unwittingly, you will cause the new widow pain.

With bereavement the question of grief – and time – is going to be an issue. Society in general – and that means people like you and me – seems to have an in-built expectation that a widow will have got over her grief in a matter of months. You will often hear someone say, 'But he died nearly a year ago, she must have got over it by now!'

Bereavement counsellors know that the reality is rather different. Two or more years may pass before a healthy mourning is completed.

I remember a girl – for some reason I always thought of her as a girl, although she was in her early forties when I saw her. She was a musician, the only child of what seemed to have been a rather difficult and over-bearing father who appeared to have loved her angrily. He had died nearly five years before I saw her. She said to me – as other people have said – 'I feel as if I've got a lid on top of me and my feelings. I can't go forward, somehow; I just can't get on with my life'.

She had worked through most of her grief, but there were some aspects of the love–hate relationship that she just could not come to terms with until she had been able to identify them and then to talk about them. I can only assume she did this satisfactorily, because at the conclusion of one meeting, when I was about to discuss the date for our next appointment, she said 'Oh, well, that's all right. I don't need to make another date. I don't need to see you again, but thanks very much'.

I left her, feeling... well, feeling surprised and a little rejected – but I had to abide by her feelings, her decision.

Another client who presented some time after the death of his wife was Dickie. He was slight and shy; very diffident and unsure of himself. He told me he was an accountant, but eventually it emerged that he was really just a book-keeper; he had a low-paid job in a big firm and he was pretty isolated in his small department.

Not surprisingly, perhaps, his wife – from the photographs he eventually produced – had been a big, buxom, decisive lady. It appeared she had had huge vitality and a host of friends. Her death had been devastating for Dickie, leaving him totally bereft. It had also been highly inconvenient and almost bordered on being selfish – but, of course, she couldn't help dying.

Dickie had managed much of his subsequent life with great courage. He had learned how to take the washing to his local launderette and to brave the sniggers of the women who thronged it. He could manage the vacuum cleaner and had learnt how to empty it, and he had mastered the intricacies of both the microwave and the video recorder.

He still had some hurt and anger with the hospital. 'That nurse,' he said, 'put all Viv's effects into a black plastic bag – all that was left of her, just thrown into a bin liner and slung at me with a "Here, you'd better take these with you." I ask you! A bin liner! How could they! All that was left of Viv. Couldn't they rate her a bit better than that, worth something more than just a black plastic bag!'

His pain was very raw. But there was more; another, deeper pain. Some years before her illness had begun to manifest itself, his wife, his idol whom he had put upon a pedestal, had come before the courts on a charge of shoplifting. The second time, she had been fined, with a recommendation to seek medical help. It had all been very, very painful and humiliating. Dickie had gone into the witness box and defended her, but the memory still hurt so badly and was one of the things which made him say, 'I can't get on with things. I'm all tangled up'.

He was rather evasive about what he meant by 'getting on with things' and I was left to guess. I guessed that once he had got rid of his anger, he wanted to know if it was all right if he could give himself permission to think of marrying again. The subject was never actually mentioned, but the next time we met I worked on this assumption.

Had it not been so, had I been wrong, he would have corrected me at once: 'No, no, that's not what I meant at all.' So we spent most of our session discussing the reactions of various members of the family should he remarry. His own mother lived in a home and half the time did not know which day of the week it was. His only brother lived a hundred miles away, busy with a farm and his own family. Viv had a much younger sister, who seemed to have the same vitality and liveliness. 'Think she's got her eye on me, sometimes.' Dickie confessed. 'And what do you feel about that?' I asked. He laughed. 'She's never married, don't quite know why. But, she'd be a bit too much of a handful for me!' We discussed the practical difficulties of a man in his late fifties meeting someone suitable. When I mentioned a Marriage Bureau, he was shocked. 'Oh, no, I was thinking of something much warmer!'

It was with no great surprise that I received his phone call a few days later, cancelling our next appointment. Something had come up; he was very sorry but he would be a bit too busy to see me again just at the moment. He thanked me warmly for the help; said he felt much better. So I knew he had finally gone flying off into the sunshine, nearly five years after Viv's death.

Dickie may have come to terms with his problem after four or five years. We had met about half a dozen times. But in counselling, how many sessions do you need to have with a client? This is like asking, 'How long is a piece of string?'

I often think of Alf and his love story. When I think back, I wonder if either I was a total failure as a counsellor or if in just one session I gave him all the help he needed to resolve his grief for himself.

I could hear the stairs creaking as he came down to open the door when I rang his bell. He was a man with thick grey hair and a kindly face. I hardly had time to give him my name before he collapsed into tears. At almost a hand gallop we rushed up to his flat, through the living room which – at speed – seemed to me comfortable and orderly, before making home base in the kitchen.

Between us, on the table, was a roll of paper towels. Alf was talking non-stop and I was totally confused, deluged under the shower of words and feelings. Finally, I managed to grasp the situation, exert some control and make some sense and order. I gathered some facts, Alf calmed down, and he became more coherent.

His wife, Carlotta, had died some months before. She had died in the same hospital and from the same illness as my own husband. For a moment, I felt uneasy.

Alf was devastated by her death. I hardly needed to invite him to tell me about her; he could barely wait to let the story all pour out. So we sat together in his kitchen, and he pulled endless folds from the towel roll. And, in my turn, so did I, because we cried together in the end.

Although Alf had spent much of his childhood in London, his family came from Suffolk. He had married, early in the war, and sent his wife back to his family for safety.

> 'Well, I'd been in the army, like, hadn't I? That Itie bit and Anzio and advancing... Cor! Rough old bit that were. But we came home in the end.'

After five years away, he had walked in through the front door of his little cottage to find his wife – and two babies, one being breast-fed.

> 'Well, I says, I see you bin doing your own bleeding kind of war work, ain't you? Then you can bleeding do your bit of peace work, gal!'

He had not even hung up his coat. He simply picked up his gunny bag, turned on his heel and left the house. He came back to London and shacked up with an army mate who was doing some building work. After the war, what with bomb damage and neglect, there was plenty of work to be had.

'So, there we was, painting this restaurant – well, more a caff really. And there was this girl, doing the waitress bit. Right proper little smasher she was, too.' I watched his calloused hands describe an invisible hour-glass. 'Cor, she didn't half go at me! "Mind your great muddy boots, I don't want you mucking up my nice clean floor!" "Blimey!" I said. "Wot you expect me to do, walk on me hands or summink?" And she was laughing like. I could sort of tell. "Just keep on them dust sheets!" she said. Well, the next day, I says, sarky like, "Well, where's me red carpet, then?" She tossed them curls. "Cheek!" but I kind of knew she didn't mind. Well, the next day I says, "Have you got a bloke, a steady bloke what you're going with?" And when she says, "No, but what's it got to do with you?" I says "Well, what about you and me going to the flicks one night?" "Well", she says, "I got no bloke, but I got to get home, to me Mum. But what about a cup of tea?" So, we had tea togevver, and the next night we went to the movies. Never touched her, I didn't. Didn't seem right, like. Any road, we was walking home and she says, "Better come for tea tomorrow, meet my Dad and Mum!"'

Alf looked at me, tears running down his kindly, lined face. 'And a'terwards, I'd say to her, "Cor, you weren't half a fast worker" and, Lotta'd say, "Knew we were going to get married, right from the start. Didn't seem much point in hanging about."'

Carlotta was that rather odd thing, a pure Italian who had never set foot outside England. Her family had come over during the thirties, and all the children had been born in London. There was considerable opposition to the marriage to begin with, and not the least reason was Carlotta's previous experience...

'War time!' Alf's massive, navvy's fist crashed onto the table. 'Don't give me no wartime! Right, proper bastard he were, wartime or no!'

At some point, Carlotta had met and married an American service man. When peace came, it had been a case of 'Well, thank you kindly, Ma'm' and off to his little wife back home. She had suffered all the humiliation and pain and betrayal of discovering that she had had a bigamous marriage. And yet...she had met and instantly trusted Alf.

No wonder we cried together over the kitchen table and into our paper towels. They had been married over forty years when she died. They had had five children and had fostered a couple more along the way. They had fought and quarrelled – 'Cor, she didn't have red hair for nuffink, did my Lotta!' – and laughed and loved each other with a fierce vitality.

'Proper fast worker' he reminisced. 'And that bugger, that con-man. Came bleeding sniffing round after her, a good many years back. I told him, I did, "She don't want you, you got no place here. You just hop it. Had your chance with her and you blew it. You get on your bike, my fine friend."'

Alf never drew breath. He never stopped crying. All thoughts of the boundary of an hour-long meeting vanished under the bombardment of emotion. How could it not? I was sharing a love story.

When I went to keep our next appointment there was a note: 'Sorry, called away. Unexpected.' I wrote confirming my telephone number, asking Alf to ring to make another date, but he never did. I was left wondering. I just hope I gave him the help he needed.

3

Unfortunately, there are some people whom it is very difficult to help at all, for some in-built 'life reason'. George was one such person.

A major bereavement is accompanied by a profound stirring of the emotions. However painful this may be, that pain is also stimulating, there is a sense of excitement, a feeling of being 'on a high'. For the first time, perhaps, in an otherwise rather mundane life, the widow is the absolute centre of attention and, despite all her shock, pain and confusion, she is enjoying this enormously.

Her family, without necessarily realising the conflicting signals they are picking up, may react with strained patience: 'She does make a meal of things, doesn't she!'

Perhaps there was an element of this with George...

However one may wish to phrase this, George had low mental ability. He was not naturally very intelligent and had been a slow learner at school. He had enjoyed his primary school, but the greater demands of secondary school had been too much for him. So he 'copped out', truanted regularly and fell further and further behind in his academic work. He was just literate, in that he could find out the television programmes by looking in the paper, but he never read easily enough to read a book for pleasure. He was sent to a secondary school he hadn't wanted to go to and I think he had set his face against school from the beginning. He was not bullied. Although he was not very tall, he must have been a big lad and he had grown into a strong man, with huge, broad shoulders.

Because of his truanting, he fell behind in his work. Ignorance compounded his natural slowness. He felt more and more inadequate, and finally emerged in the employment market with practically nothing to offer any employer but his strength.

He still lived at home with his parents. His father had been in the RAF during the war. George was extremely proud of him, and showed me photographs and newspaper cuttings of a medal presentation ceremony, on my first visit. For the rest of his life, his father had worked for British Transport. It was particularly sad that, after only a year or two of his retirement, he had died.

George was devastated. His father and he had been very close. I looked at the photograph and saw a man with a plain but kindly face. He seemed to have been very good to the boy. They used to go down to their local pub for a couple of pints every weekend, where they met up with a crowd of his father's cronies. Both men shared an interest in the local football team and occasionally still went train-spotting together.

George seemed to have no friends. The only work he was able to get was low paid, unskilled labouring work. He had previously been a cellar man in a local off-licence and, although he said he had left it to help at home with his father's last illness, I began to have doubts. George talked very freely about his life, and it appeared that, when he made one of his frequent job-changes, the pattern was always the same. 'Someone told me off, so I thumped them!' I started to feel slightly uneasy.

Poor George, he was so lonely. Although he lived with his mother – and there was a married sister with her family not far away – he was terribly isolated. It seemed as if his father was the only person who had ever been kind to him, or had taken any real interest in his life. George's grief was very raw.

Over the next few weeks, I began to see that he had no wish at all to give up his grief. 'I shall never get over it! Never!' and his vast, clenched fist hammered on the chair arm. 'Don't matter what you say, I shan't get over it!' It sounded very like a statement of intent.

The anniversary of his father's birthday was the following month. Now, anniversaries are always terribly difficult times in a bereavement; the first Christmas, the date of a wedding, and that most major one of all, the first anniversary of the death. No one can possibly help looking back and thinking, 'This time last year...' However, it becomes cumbersome to say 'This time the year before last...'

George was preparing a grand emotional outing for this particular anniversary. 'I shall cry all day', he announced. I had been glad, for his sake, that he cried so easily and did not bottle up his emotions. 'I shall visit Dad'. 'Visit?' I was slightly jolted and George looked at me, with disdain.

'Course I'll visit him! Only right and proper. Got the flowers ordered already. I might take some sandwiches up to the Cemetery, make a day out with him'.

'Oh, I see.'

'Even that silly cow what lives next door, she thought it proper. Said to my Mum the other day, "Poor George. It's always hard and a boy does need a father..."'

It was only then that I recognised the note in his voice. It was excitement. His feelings for his father were absolutely genuine, but he was enjoying every moment of them. In an essentially rather drab and lonely life, for the first time he was the centre of interest, he was attracting attention, and he had absolutely no intention whatsoever of giving up his grief. He even had me as a captive audience for an hour every week. I had nothing to offer for a future that in any way compared with his heady interest and so, really, is it any wonder he did not want to give up his feelings?

Another person who could not give up easily was Gabriella. She held on to feelings and property and people with great tenacity.

She was a beautiful woman in her late fifties; tall and graceful with all the elegance of a pedigree greyhound. Like such dogs, she had a thin nervousness, but in her it manifested itself in a highly exaggerated form.

When I first saw her, she was almost incoherent; she stuttered, because her words were too quick for her tongue, and I noticed that the long, thin hand lying on the arm of her chair was trembling.

Visiting Gabriella had its practical difficulties. She had a Siamese cat called Orpheus, with a highly developed personality. Luckily, I do not have a cat phobia. Unfortunately, however, Orpheus took a great fancy to me, and would leap on to my lap and lie, sprawled, painfully kneading my thighs with his claws. Gabriella became uneasy, and spent much time trying to coax him to come to *her*, and not for the sake of my feelings; she was slightly jealous of the attention he paid to me. With the perversity of his kind, Orpheus refused to move; this was hardly restful or conductive to successful counselling. But what could I do?

However, finally we all sorted ourselves out, and I heard something about her first marriage to the father of her two children. Their divorce had been of the bitterest kind, the sort where only the lawyers benefit. Gabriella was still involved so much in such feelings of jealousy and outrage I began to wonder about her second marriage. However, she seemed to have been genuinely fond of Jeremy.

He had died six months before, and they had been married for about three years. 'It was rather rushed through,' she explained. 'To regularise the situation when he knew how ill he was.' After a while, I understood what she meant. She had married him, knowing that he had had treatment for cancer. When the cancer recurred, she wanted to be the legal wife – and widow – so that she would qualify for the pensions.

She had looked after him and supported him quite excellently. She had seen him buried with honour and sincerely mourned him, felt the pain of missed laughter, shared understanding and companionship.

For all that she was a highly intelligent and cultured woman, Gabriella was deficient in the quality of detachment. Clearly, she did not hear what she was saying to me at the beginning of one session when she exploded to me.

'That woman' – by then I had learned 'That Woman' was her first husband's new wife – 'That woman! Do you know what she's done now?'

Apparently, the step-mother had rung the younger daughter to invite her for a meal and had left a message to that effect on Gabriella's answerphone.

'I will not have it!' I realised Gabriella was a very forceful woman. 'I will not tolerate it! How dare she! I will not have my telephone sullied and made dirty by her voice!'

I realised Gabriella was perfectly serious. I also realised that here were muddied waters and deep marriage issues for which I was not equipped. I could only suggest she sought additional help from another agency.

Whenever I saw Gabriella, however, these issues surfaced, like jagged rocks showing up at ebb tide, and gradually I learned how to paddle round them. I sensed, too, that there was something deeper, causing her obsession with money and possessions, which made any kind of rejection utterly intolerable for her.

One day she began to talk about her parents and her childhood. Her mother had died when Gabriella was six years old.

'She died from tuberculosis. Funny, isn't it? It's such an old-fashioned word, it's an obsolete illness today. But before the war there wasn't much doctors could do. It's amazing to think of the strides medicine has made in my lifetime, all the drugs they've invented...

'My mother was such a fun person – she was beautiful and elegant and she loved having a daughter. I can remember how she used to go shopping and she'd take me with her. She'd buy wonderful dresses – my parents were very sociable, and they entertained a great deal, so lovely evening dresses – and then she'd buy something pretty for me...'

But the disease had manifested itself. Her mother became bed-ridden. Because of the fear of infection, Gabriella was not allowed to climb up onto the high bed, snuggle up to her mother, still beautiful in a satin-and-lace nightie, shoulders covered by a spider-web thin shawl. She had had to stand on the far side of the room, with her nanny's hand on her shoulders.

One day she was not allowed to go in to see her mother. The next day her father took her into the cold dining room. The maids had cleaned it, polished the furniture. 'I've never been able to bear the smell of furniture polish,' she said. Her father said, 'Your mother has died. It's all very sad, but now we'll never talk about it again...'

And, for fifty-two years, she never had.

It was at about this stage in her counselling that I knew Gabriella had decided to get rid of me. She did not say so, of course, but she began to make remarks like, 'There must be so many other people who need your help; I shouldn't be taking up your time like this...'

She also decided she needed money and that she must get a job. Being highly efficient she soon found one.

I suggested we wait a week or two before making another appointment, to give her time to settle down at work. But she never contacted me again.

❀ ❀ ❀ ❀ ❀ ❀ ❀ ❀ ❀ ❀

The social aspects of widowhood presents problems, especially to widows who are completing their tasks of mourning, and many people may not be aware of them.

In trying to understand – and indeed, to adjust to the difficulties of becoming a widow – the relationship of that widow to the society in which she lives is an extremely important if neglected area. How does a widow rebuild her life, how does she re-enter society in her new role, and how will society react to her? On the one hand, there is the question of life inside her home, and then there is the question of the emotions and her life outside the house.

Perhaps Annie is one of the best examples I can find to illustrate these dilemmas. When I first saw her, she was in her mid-fifties and her husband had died five years before. She had asked for counselling on the advice of one of her daughters. Annie said, 'I just feel I can't get on with my life properly'.

Anne came originally from a remote Highland village, and she was both gentle and dignified. She had married when she was twenty and there were two sons and two daughters from the marriage.

Three of the children were settled and married and the younger boy, then still living at home, was engaged to be married. She had a host of grandchildren, and it was obviously a happy and caring family. They all saw each other regularly. In the early days of Annie's bereavement, the children had provided all the social support she needed. But, as she worked through her grief, she felt she wanted something more.

Annie had a little job as a luncheon waitress to an exclusive firm. She enjoyed the work, and it was apparent that the Directors were all very fond of her and valued her. She was an extremely pretty woman, in a plump, motherly way, with the most delightful laugh and an impish twinkle in her eye.

One of the things she missed was, quite simply, masculinity. She was, after all, with a husband and two sons, used to the company of men; muddy football gear, fishing tackle in the hall, shirts to be ironed. She was used to cooking in quantities to satisfy the hunger of four growing children. She accepted that this part of her life had gone, but she still missed it. Most of her friends were married women, but Annie did not particularly want to go out only in the company of women. After all, previously, most of her social activity had been as part of a pair. She had no wish to live a riotous life, to paint the town red, but she did not want just to sit at home and watch television every evening.

When James was alive, they used quite often to go down to the local pub on Saturday night, just for an hour or two, to meet with a group of friends and perhaps play darts or crib. With four children to bring up on small wages, it was not a wild evening. It was just fun, and she missed it.

She had not been back. It is extremely difficult for a woman, especially a shy, middle-aged and respectable woman, to go into a pub alone – and often even the publican himself will make it clear that he does not welcome single women who may be on the lookout for whomever they can pick up. Yet a local is just that, a centre of social life.

Annie had gone once, with a couple, and had met the old crowd. They had all been delighted to see her, been kind and welcoming. She was getting over James' death, and found she could talk about him quite naturally, could accept the clumsy sympathy. But she was not entirely happy.

She had not wanted to be a 'passenger' and, although she had never bought a round of drinks in her life, she had clutched her money and steeled herself to do so when suddenly the 'drinking school' grew too big. She could have afforded a round of three drinks, but eight was far too much for her resources. She felt awkward and uncomfortable.

The husband of the couple she had come with, relaxed by a few drinks, sat slightly apart, talking to Annie. He had been a special friend of James'; they had played bowls together. In his own way, the man was grieving for his friend. Annie and he enjoyed reminiscing, laughing over the past. Then, as Annie put it, 'His wife became ever so funny with me. Afterwards, I felt uncomfortable with her. It was ever so sad – we'd known them since our kids were all babies... it was never the same again between us. When I meet her out shopping now, she hardly talks to me. I've not really seen either of them since that evening...'

However unreasonable it may seem, one can understand why the wife became 'funny'. She was simply alarmed and jealous, and the straightforward Annie could not understand this. She was hurt and upset. The invitation was not repeated.

Annie's first, brave attempt to get back into normal life turned out to be a great setback. She was responding naturally to her own driving life-force, but society was putting up barriers – was saying, in effect, 'So far and no further'. Annie was a woman, a relatively young woman, but a woman without a man in a world largely designed by and for couples. She was a threat.

She would certainly never have considered an affair, nor was she looking for one. I doubt whether she even wished to re-marry. Like all of us, she was programmed by a certain social conditioning. As a girl, she went looking for someone to love. She found him, married him, and when, thirty-five years later he had died and she was alone again, she had no other social experience on which to fall back. What she knew *then* was totally inappropriate to her current situation and needs.

The classic advice given generally at this point in life is 'Take up a hobby; find a new interest'. No doubt it is very good advice, but it is often difficult to follow. There is something very bleak about the necessity to find a new interest. A good many people who have been absorbed in working and bringing up a family for many years have had neither the time nor the money for hobbies and outside interests.

There is no solution, or certainly no easy solution. When they least feel like doing so, when all they want is the reassurance of the familiar, new widows have to learn new behaviour. That they find it very hard, and may not necessarily even mention it, does not mean the problem does not exist. If one is to try to help a widow, it is essential to understand some of these problems.

In Annie's case, the common bromide on offer – 'Bingo' or 'Singles Holidays' were beyond Annie's capabilities. She had never been to the cinema alone in her life and found the idea extremely alarming. The other interest she and her husband had shared was Old Tyme Dancing... it is hard to imagine any activity more demanding of a partner! She would certainly never have even considered going alone – and who can blame her? She and James had once been on a package tour to Spain and, although she considered this, she was alarmed. 'I'd be a bit scared, and if I felt like that I don't think it would be much of a holiday, do you?' She was also wondering if she could afford it. Very few widows are wealthy, and although Annie could manage, her resources were slender.

Even for women who are more sophisticated and financially better off than Annie, there are still areas of social rejection. Formal dinner parties are a classic problem because an extra man is needed to make up the numbers. Widows get left out.

Very subtly, society defines widows, and thereby creates a special sub-group. We all do this collectively, and unconsciously, and it can be heard in that most powerful medium – our unconsidered and everyday speech.

A friend of mine was talking about her brother, who is an attractive scamp. She said... 'and he's got a new lady friend,' adding – after some brief, internal scan – 'she's a widow'. Now, had this woman been a spinster, the matter would never have been mentioned.

In a popular radio 'soap opera,' one character was recently referred to as the 'The Widow Woodford'. It was entirely accepted; no one queried it. I doubt if any but a tiny proportion of the listening public would even have noticed. Had the roles been reversed, would her husband have been referred to as 'The Widower Woodford'? I doubt it very much.

The title 'Widow' was quite common in the country district where I grew up, and it may still be so today. In many social groupings, it is considered natural that a man whose wife has died will remarry. However, there is also a strong and widespread expectation, if unspoken, that a widow should remain chaste and faithful, even after death. I remember when I was a child one of my cousins wished to marry a war-widow. The great aunts twittered with outrage and disapproval, not because the girl was unsuitable in any other way, simply because she was a widow.

There is a long, narrative poem by John Masefield, called 'The Widow in the Bye-Street' and we all accept the term in that context, quite naturally. Recently, I was listening to a radio programme on the founding of the Baptist Movement, and several times the founder was referred to as The Widow Betty Wallace.

The word widow is linked to other things. There is the Black Widow Spider — and that association can hardly be said to be happy, good or pleasant. There is a famous champagne which has the nickname of 'The Widow'. Printers and compositors have a special meaning for the word, to indicate an unacceptable, single line at the start of a new page. We refer to someone whose hair grows in a certain way as having 'a widow's peak'. Although the colloquial term 'widow's weeds' may now be obsolete, most people will understand the meaning — and whoever wants 'weeds'? Probably the most famous person to be entitled 'Widow' was Queen Victoria who was, of course, known popularly as 'The Widow of Windsor'.

In our everyday speech, we show what we feel about widows
– and none of these feelings is positive or complimentary.

❦ ❦ ❦ ❦ ❦ ❦ ❦ ❦ ❦

If we, that is, the whole of society, infer so much about widows
and thereby influence widows so much, how much more will
the children be affected? This book is primarily addressing the
problems of women who become widows. But if a wife's role
has changed, so has it changed for a child who, in the play-
ground, has become different from its peers and is subject to
the jibe 'You haven't got a Daddy any more, have you?'
Counselling children is very specialised and not part of this
book. But remember, children need to talk, to be listened to,
too.

Death can take anyone. Each person knows this, everyone
says 'Yes, of course!' But death is for someone else, a happening
on a distant hill top, taking place in someone else's front garden,
until...

There are what one might call 'special' deaths. Death by
murder, or sudden accident; suicide; death from AIDS; and also
the death of a child. These deaths produce extremely complicated and painful problems, and are not suitable for inclusion
into a general study of widowhood.

But...

The death of a parent means you are saying good-bye to
your childhood. There is no longer anyone who calls you by a
pet name, one which perhaps evolved from some babyhood
mispronunciation.

The death of your partner means you have said good-bye to
your present.

The death of a child means you have lost your future. It means... it means many things. It means, for the parents, 'Who will look after us when we are old and frail and helpless?' It means, 'Who will see that we are buried in a seemly way when our time comes?' Because of the very special problems involved in the death of a child an excellent specialist organisation has been formed which can give parents a great deal of help.[1]

Sadly, there is currently an escalation in the suicide rate. Suicide is the ultimate act of aggression, and the emotional fall-out comes to friends and family, 'Won't you be sorry when I'm gone!' Their response must always be, 'Where did we go wrong? What should we have done to prevent it?' Suicide is a very punitive act and there are enormous ramifications and complexities for the people left behind. It is always essential that help be sought from a specialist agency.

For everyone, the loss of a significant loved one means there has been a major shift in the balance of family relationships. The younger members have suddenly – and perhaps reluctantly – become 'the older generation'. Perhaps the dead mother was the person who held the family together, insisted on (boring!) family parties, and kept all the latent jealousies and hostilities at bay. With her death, all sorts of feelings errupt; violent quarrels take place, the family splits and hardly ever meets. On the other hand, sometimes people are newly drawn together, and form new and comforting bonds.

If an elderly father dies, the grief-stricken mother may retire from active life. Her son will have to assume many responsibilities, take his place among The Elder Statesmen.

---

1   The Society of Compassionate Friends.
    Head office: 53 North Street, Bristol BS3 1EN. Tel: 0117 966 5202.
    Information on local groups is available through the National Secretary.

If that son had always been rather indulged, he may well resent the demands made on him in his new role. The jealousy between his mother and his wife may come to the surface. His wife considers he is 'dancing attendance on a spoilt old woman', and the poor man retorts, 'But someone's got to look after her, see to her affairs. You know my young brother is worse than useless!' Between these conflicts, the needs of the grandchildren tend to be rather overlooked.

Perhaps this neglect is one of the reasons why, in counselling, someone will often mention the death of a grandparent. There is some old grief that has been brought back by their present loss. In other words, their feelings have been reactivated. It happens very often, and cannot be better illustrated than by an account of the beautiful Lizzie.

Lizzie was referred, with her permission, by her step-mother. The girl's father had died, suddenly but not entirely unexpectedly. 'Liz has gone completely to pieces. She can't stop crying, she can't eat and she can't sleep'. He had been something of an invalid due to the injuries he had received about fifteen years before when his first wife died. There was a note, explaining that Liz's mother had been killed when a drunk driver had ploughed into a bus queue. She had died, instantly, and her husband had been terribly injured.

The message I left on Lizzie's answer phone brought no response, so I followed up with a letter suggesting she might like to telephone me. It was perhaps some two months later before she could bring herself to do so.

Lizzie was extremely dynamic, intelligent and gifted. She and another girl ran an extremely successful business. Liz was altogether a high-powered, modern miss. At our first meeting she tilted her chin up to me, showing her long, elegant neck, and declared 'I've quite got over my mother's death, you know.

It was such a long time ago. All this upset over Dad has got nothing to do with her!' When I asked if she had ever talked about her mother's death, she was quite surprised. 'Why should I?'

We discussed her father, their relationship, his re-marriage and his death. I asked what she felt about the driver of the car. She was vague. 'He was really very young. Rather good-looking. I saw him in court, of course.' 'And what did you think about the sentence?' Liz shook her head. 'It just seemed rather awful to send someone to prison. I remember walking out into the sunshine and thinking, "He can't do this".'

It seemed an inappropriate reaction about someone who had killed your mother! Lovely Liz, so honest and brave, came true in the end. She would say, 'When my mother died', until one day I said, 'When your mother was murdered!' She looked at me in amazement. 'But, Liz, surely that was what happened? The man had been warned by his mates in the pub he wasn't fit to drive. But he did, quite deliberately!'

She had never been able to think of her mother's death in those terms before, and found it extremely hard to acknowledge them now. We considered various violent deaths. We agreed that cars are potentially dangerous, particularly in the hands of drunk drivers. We agreed that morally, if a drunk driver kills someone, then they have committed murder.

Liz never seemed to have had time to grieve for her mother and, at the time of the death, there was no one to help her. Her father had been in hospital for nearly a year. Liz had been about eighteen or nineteen at the time. She had a couple of younger sisters to look after – both in their early teens. Her mother's twin sister, always nervous and highly-strung, had become extremely neurotic and could provide neither support nor practical help. Her father had a much older sister, living three hundred miles away. She did what she could, but she had commitments of her own. Liz had to cope with everything.

Eventually, and with the help of a good many packets of paper tissues, we talked about her relationship with her mother, and all the unfinished conflicts present in most teenage relationships. Finally, I felt it was safe to ask, 'What would you feel now, if you had him, that driver, in your power? If he was lying helpless on the floor here? What would you want to do?' She lifted her hand, made the motion of plunging a dagger and I saw a circular movement. 'The knife?' She nodded. 'Right in? Round and round? And blood? Lots of blood?'

Liz nodded, then 'Great gouts of it. Spouting. All over the place. I'd kill him, and kill and then I'd kill all over again!'

She started to cry. I held her, felt her sweating, and just had to wait until she ran out of tears. Then it was nearly over. I think I saw her twice more, but by then she had rid herself of pain she had tucked away and endured for fifteen years.

Pain is a word that seems to have appeared frequently in this book. We all react positively to physical pain. If there is a lump of grit lodged in the base of one's foot, one can hardly wait for privacy to take off the shoe and peel it out with a finger nail. It is almost worth having this discomfort for the relief that comes afterwards.

The pain of bereavement has a use. A woman may say to herself – if to nobody else – 'I must have loved him very much, far more than I ever realised when he was alive, otherwise I wouldn't be so upset now!' Some of the more prickly areas in a difficult relationship are neutralised and the pain itself can be a comfort. However, sometimes pain leaches inwards and that will certainly cause problems.

Angela was a pretty woman, like a small porcelain figure. She had been married for thirty years and her husband had died very suddenly after a complicated operation. Angela was threatening to sue the doctor for negligence, but luckily family counsel and good sense prevailed.

Angela had enough talent as a painter to be accepted for art school, but half-way through her course she had met, then married, her David. There had been some family opposition to the marriage, largely because David was so much older. But Angela had exactly what she wanted; a wealthy husband, whom she adored, and three healthy, intelligent successful children.

She was obviously a very capable woman, and ran her household and life with great efficiency. Indeed, I often thought she would have made an excellent Managing Director. Yet she seemed oddly naive about some things. When I asked her if her finances were in order, she looked surprised. 'I suppose so. I leave all that to the solicitors and the bank'.

There had always been money, so she expected money to be there still. It had never occurred to her that her comfortable life-style might change after David's death; a car for him, a car for her, a runabout for the children. She had absolutely no idea about budgeting, apart from her housekeeping allowance, no idea what it cost to run the house, and things like insurance never crossed her mind. I could only hope she was being given good advice.

I saw Angela, on and off, for many months. She had a sister in New York; she and David had a holiday home in Spain. Angela was constantly flitting round the world. I began to wonder if the reason she did not seem to be moving on, working through her grief, was due to our intermittent sessions.

One day she gave me a clue. She fingered the pendant she always wore. It had been David's last present and I had noticed whenever she was upset that she clutched it, as if for comfort.

'It's awful, this pain. And yet, you know, in some ways I like it. I'm all right outside – laughing and cheerful. All my friends say how wonderfully I'm coping. Then I come home and go inside myself and cry. And then, I feel close to David.' She paused. 'I just want to put the clock back.'

When I said, 'But you can't do that, no one can do that,' she said nothing, but set her jaw. She looked remarkably like a small, wilful child!

Very gradually I realised that, not only could she not do so, she simply would not recognise that her marriage was only an interlude – a long and profound one, but still only an interlude in her life. It had been her full-time occupation; she expected it to go on for ever and ever and, when it had ended, she was extremely put out.

She found all these emotions very bewildering and frightening so, being a sensible and practical person, she had looked round for help. The help she wanted was not for the resolution of her grief. She wanted someone to be an emotional baby-sitter, to reassure her when her feelings frightened her.

We struggled on for some weeks and then I gradually withdrew from the sessions. Angela was decidedly irritated by my going but we managed to talk it through, to part with affection and as good friends.

Never believe that bereavement is easy and straightforward!

4

It would be possible to go on and on with stories, because all human life is here. These only highlight some of the problems most often encountered with the bereaved, but we seem to have moved a long way from our original picture of a gentle widow, sniffing slightly and sipping a cup of tea with you.

However, as you sit, chatting together, may I please urge you NOT to say certain things. Please, please don't say – however well-intentioned you are – 'My dear, I do know just what you are going through'. You don't. It is an outrageously hurtful and affronting statement, because what that widow has lost is an emotional intimacy which was entirely unique.

Now, emotional intimacy is difficult to define, so imagine a situation where a middle-aged couple is giving a party to celebrate some family occasion. Everyone is there, including Auntie Maud and Uncle Fred. We all have them, the tiresome, elderly relations.

Serving food behind the buffet, the wife hears Uncle Fred's voice above all the other chatter, and she knows, quite certainly, that he has had two drinks too many. Uncle Fred will hit his stride, launch into his war-time reminiscences – 'Eh, lad, when I was with Bomber Command, the tales I could tell…' and once Uncle Fred gets started he is capable of carrying on for hours! Across the room, she manages to catch her husband's eye and nods towards Uncle Fred's corner. Her husband looks, then nods back to her. As he moves off to deal with Uncle Fred, he winks at his wife. Now, they haven't spoken, but there has been total communication between husband and wife, involving all kinds of complicated family relationships and dynamics. And this kind of understanding between two people is only achieved by living in domestic harmony together for many years.

When her husband dies, that woman will miss the communication and understanding, at all kinds of levels and in a million different ways. The widow has lost all that private love she shared with her husband: sitting-up all night together with a seriously ill child; the tiny ritual of Christmas, nothing very significant, but things like putting out food for the reindeer on Christmas Eve. Things we do not talk about, because they are funny and private and we fear we may be laughed at. The pet names they had for each other when they made love – all gone and forever.

She will also know that it can never be replaced, because even if she were to re-marry, it would be different. For an outsider to say, 'I understand what you are going through' is, therefore, an outrageous and cruel statement.

If you feel you must make some comment, try saying something like 'I do know this is such a difficult (or lonely) or (painful) time'. You might add, 'It does get better'. It is true, but she probably won't believe you, yet the words may stick in the back of her mind to give her some comfort and hope.

Your widow may burst into tears every time you see her, and go on doing so, week after week. Please don't, however gently you say it, remark, 'You really must try to pull yourself together, my dear. You mustn't give way like this!'

The trouble is, she can't pull herself together, much as she would like to do so. She has been invaded by terrifying and powerful feelings which she has never experienced before. She is bewildered and alarmed by herself. She has no control or understanding of her feelings. It is hardly helpful to ask her to pull herself together when not only is she totally incapable of doing so but she may also, temporarily, have lost the identity of that self.

Don't say, 'You mustn't cry like this. George wouldn't have liked to see you carrying on so much!'

This remark is very often made, and it is rather a silly one. For one thing, George was her husband, not yours. You don't really know what he would have said; he might have been highly gratified that his wife is so upset and is mourning him so deeply. For another thing, George is now dead. What he would or would not have said is rather irrelevant.

Don't say, to a woman who is weeping desperately, 'You mustn't cry so much. If you go on like this, you'll make yourself ill'. Tears are a release of emotion, after all, and tears can be healing in themselves. And remember, with her husband's death, the widow has also had to confront her own mortality.

We all rush through our lives with the knowledge of death but the belief it will not happen to us. Death is for other people. The implication that, by doing something she can't help doing, she is going actually to make herself ill is, therefore, doubly terrifying. You may feel much better for making this bracing kind of remark, but it will not help her!

And, please, don't say, 'You really must get a grip on yourself, dear. Think of the children!'

Now, the widow is a good mother, she loves her children deeply. But for the first time in their lives, they are faintly irrelevant to her. She feels slightly guilty about them already, and increasing her guilt is not actually going to be comforting.

We all make remarks like this, generally with the best of intentions. We make them because we ourselves do not feel very comfortable in the face of raw and ugly grief. *We* may feel better, but the effect on a new widow will only be to make her feel more isolated and frightened. If she is not allowed to express her feelings and her fears, she will hide away, cry in private – or not go out and she may turn her feelings inwards, not talk about them. But the feelings will not go away.

So, *do* remember – there is nothing you can do to help or take away her pain. Grief is a path we have to walk alone.

If a woman looks at you, her face ravaged, looking ten years older than she really is, her reddened eyes filling yet again with tears and she says, 'It's so awful, this feeling, this pain. I wake up each morning and I don't know how to get through the day'; or, rather disturbingly, she says, 'Life simply isn't worth living, I just don't see the point of going on...' – well, realistically, what can you say?

She will make you feel inadequate, and the truth is, you *are* inadequate. It is not a comfortable feeling. It is one of the reasons why many people cross the road to avoid a new widow.

I have done it, and it has happened to me; a friend, waving, making signs she was in a hurry, giving signals she would telephone me soon – but I knew! Widows are over-sensitive. To be avoided simply makes them feel that much more hurt, more isolated, the more alone – and less likely to share their feelings.

Inadequacy and embarrassment are powerful emotions. They are both also highly uncomfortable feelings, and they both give us a wish for flight, to get away.

There is nothing you can do to take the pain away from a widow, but you can give sympathy, and time. You can listen. Everyone can listen – and I mean *really* listen, not merely make your silence a short emotional gap before donating your own comments.

❧ ❧ ❧ ❧ ❧ ❧ ❧ ❧ ❧ ❧

Sooner or later I think almost everyone I have ever counselled has said something like, 'He was my best friend, you know;' 'He was my husband, but he was my friend, too'; 'He was someone I could always talk to'. If you have had that relationship, and find it has gone, it is extremely hard to accept you will never have that closeness again.

We seem to have come a long, long way from our original picture of that little widow, grey and gentle, dabbing an occasional tear with her small hanky. Not everyone will feel the emotions I have described, but most people will have experienced them in some way or another.

Bereavement is a good deal more ugly, violent and painful than many of us might have supposed. Grief is also a very complex process. It is unique. It is personal. It is totally individual, and yet everyone resolves their grief in the same way.

This process was first charted by Sigmund Freud, and he called it The Four Tasks of Mourning, labelling the stages through which everyone must go before they have resolved their grief. I rather prefer his other phrase 'Grief Work', because grieving *is* very hard work, and often, particularly in the early days of bereavement, almost a full-time, twenty-four-hour-a-day job.

The first task is to confront the reality of death. This may sound so obvious as to be trite, something one can skip over. But, just consider for a moment...

You hear of the sudden death of someone who, while not necessarily close to you, is nevertheless part of your everyday life. It might be your postman, or the man who ran the local paper shop – and you may well hear yourself exclaiming, 'Old Bob! Dead? But I saw him – only a couple of weeks ago and he was all right then! Well, well! Old Bob! Dead? I simply can't believe it!' And there it is, that phrase, those key words, 'I can't believe it'.

I am sure that no one who has ever had to arrange a funeral has not, just for a moment, paused and thought, 'this is all like a bad dream, I can't believe I'm having to do this'. There may even come a nightmare fantasy that the dead person will walk in, and you find everything has been a ghastly mistake and misunderstanding. And when that person finds their funeral is being arranged they will be extremely angry! There are occasionally very extreme cases where the relict simply refuses to believe in the death at all and will not allow any funeral to take place, but fortunately these are very rare.

Perhaps this sense of disbelief can be put into more mundane terms. If you have ever been out shopping and you discover that you have mislaid your keys or your purse, what do you do? You look for them, of course! You turn out your handbag, rummage through the shopping basket, pat all your pockets. You look on the shop counter, all across the floor, over the doorstep, down the pavement. You retrace your steps, come back to the till, in mounting panic, start the search through handbag, basket, pockets, all over again. You have lost something very important, and so – you look for it.

If we can search for keys and a purse so ardently, and with an increasing sense of disbelief – 'I can't have lost it! I had it only a moment ago, it can't just be gone!' – how much more frantic will be the search for the person we have loved.

The difference, of course, is that while keys are tangible and they can be replaced, and we can explain what we are doing so people will understand and sympathise, searching for a dead person is something we can only do inside ourselves. It is something which is done with great secrecy.

A widow knows, in her head, that her husband has died. She may or may not have actually seen his body. When a sense of disbelief comes to her, she will think back. The nurses told her that her husband had died, the doctor signed the death certificate, and the local undertakers took the body to their mortuary. She knows that all these responsible, professional people cannot be colluding in some gigantic confidence trick and a tissue of lies. But another part of her cannot believe it.

It is very scary to find you have two quite different, powerful and utterly irreconsilable sets of feelings inside you. That fear is only a step away from the added fear that you are going mad. Understandably, these are not feelings easily shared. Luckily, this terribly frightening stage passes quite normally and healthily.

When the telephone rings, the widow is no longer convinced it is her husband telephoning her. She does not 'see' him crossing the road ahead of her, does not hear his key in the lock as if he were coming back from work in the evening and she accepts he is not still sitting in his chair by the hospital bed, waiting for her visit.

But sometimes this sad stage of non-acceptance can be abnormally protracted. Perhaps the most famous person who suffered from this was Queen Victoria, who endured her widowhood so badly that it became almost a profession. She became a recluse for many years, and was, indeed, entitled The Widow of Windsor. After Prince Albert died she ordered that his dress clothes should be put out each evening and his bath was drawn. Now we can understand that she was a classic case of unresolved grief – she never even completed that first stage of mourning, accepting the reality of death.

Most people, however, are realistic. Given time, they do come to terms with the reality of death. They can bring themselves to sort out and get rid of the clothes, to distribute the personal effects. They can admit that he won't need them any more, that he will never again write with his gold pen, check his watch, and they can give them among the family as they wish.

There is no time scale within which people do or should do this, but probably a healthy time is within the first six months or so after bereavement. We all vary. People are different, they function at different times and in their own way.

The next stage is experiencing the pain of loss. There are no short cuts and no hard and fast rules. The only help you can give is understanding and affection. If she wants to do so, and if she can, let a widow talk about some of the things she misses, the things that hurt her most. They will be as different and numberless as the hairs on your hand. They will often seem, to you, such tiny matters that they hardly seem worth mentioning, but they hurt her just the same.

To this day, British Telecom sends the telephone bill in my late husband's name. For the first year, this hurt me quite desperately, I tried and tried to get the Accounts Department to change it to my name, and failed utterly. After that, I found it didn't hurt – or not very much, and so I stopped bothering about it.

Perhaps a new grandchild has been born into the family, and while the baby is a delight, the grandmother is so sad her husband didn't live long enough to see it. The husband and wife might have planted bulbs in the autumn and he died before they flowered. Although they are as beautiful and successful as the couple hoped and planned, the wife may almost hate the flowers because they are a constant reminder to her that he is no longer alive to see them.

Many widows find shopping difficult. She has been used to catering for a family, and now there is only herself. Although she can now choose food she likes and her husband hated, this freedom is accompanied by a sense of disloyalty and sadness.

She may now not trust people in some ways. Walking down a street and hearing a man's footsteps behind her, even if on the other side of the road, may make her nervous and think 'A mugger!'. This worries her, because she has always before been normally confident and not given to imaginings.

The wife may have started to knit a sweater, and now that she is a widow, the half-finished garment is a problem. Wool is expensive and she doesn't want to put it in the dustbin. She hasn't got the heart to finish it – and anyway, he is no longer alive to wear it and she doesn't feel she could bear to see the finished garment worn by a son. Perhaps she should just give it to a Charity Shop, although would anyone want to bother to complete the work? Such a tiny problem, so petty she cannot bring herself even to discuss it, but she worries about it. She may be ashamed to talk about other problems for fear of seeming silly and being laughed at.

A new widow has so many feelings churning round inside her, and these feelings take up so much of her energy, even quite small difficulties assume massive proportions.

If she shops somewhere where it is difficult to park the car, what would once have been simply irritating becomes a major problem, all too much for her. She comes tearful and panicy.

She might go to the library and finds a new book by an author she and her husband enjoyed. Automatically, she reaches out for it and thinks, 'He can read it first'. Then she remembers – her husband is no longer alive – and she will have no one to discuss it with afterwards. For a moment, she had forgotten her husband is dead – and that in itself is quite scarey. She cannot believe it is possible she forgot and she feels it is wicked to have done so. And it goes on, and on. Being so sad.

They are always what seem such silly, trivial things, and yet they matter so much. They are very real problems to a new widow. Everyone's grief is unique, and she may be afraid that if she does talk about her feelings to her friends, they will not understand. Unless they are widows themselves, she is probably right.

A common problem for both a widow and her friends is whether or not to talk about the deceased husband. Friends say, 'Well, I didn't like to mention him, you know, for fear of upsetting her. I wouldn't want to do that…' Everyone treads over-cautiously round this question as if in a desert where every cactus bush has been mined.

Some people are lucky. They have no inhibitions in talking about George. Their attitude is quite straight forward: 'Well, I knew him for over thirty years, why on earth shouldn't I talk about him? To me, it's perfectly natural to say, Do you remember…?' This may be a great help to a widow, who is longing to talk about her husband. On the other hand, she is afraid she will cry if she does so, and doesn't want to embarrass her visitor!

The solution lies within the widow herself, of course. If she can set the tone, give signals of permission that it is OK, even nice, to talk about HIM, there is no problem, particularly if she learns not to mind being seen to cry. The trouble is that very often the bereaved find this very hard to do.

❧ ❧ ❧ ❧ ❧ ❧ ❧ ❧ ❧

I have noticed quite often in bereavement counselling that a client is reluctant to tell me the name of the person who has died.

Naturally, one knows the relationship: husband, brother, sister, but often they are referred to in the third person. I have the fancy that the client is holding back the given name, that they hold it as a child holds a treasured holiday pebble, clutched safely in a tight, sticky hand, and that by actually releasing the name of the dead person they are exposing them; by sharing the name they make that person vulnerable – and perhaps make themselves vulnerable, too.

The client, by the very fact of telling me the name is giving me permission to use it – in the telling, they feel that they are performing an act of infidelity. Reluctantly, by this very act, they are acknowledging the reality of death. Sometimes, accepting the reality of death and experiencing the pain are over-lapping stages in the Tasks of Mourning.

But death is absolute. It is not something you can argue about. And life is constant. Where there is life, there is growth, and that means change. Change is either a threat or a challenge. Some widows try to stop time and create a shrine. But if they walk out of their front door, or even look out of their windows, they will see change. The tree opposite has been pollarded. The tree in the neighbouring garden has grown. Were that widow's husband to come back from the dead on a visit a year later, he would find all kinds of local differences to which she has become accustomed and yet which she is extremely reluctant to acknowledge.

Clients can go through a stage of resenting their counselling. They have a new relationship. They have a relationship with their counsellor, who is someone strange, whom their husband did not know. They may not wish to admit this, but the fact is that they are moving on with their grief work.

The pain each widow must experience in her loss will be special and unique. The stories cited are only a tiny handful of example of the most common problems a widow may find she has to face. Since they are problems that may not hitherto have occurred to her friends and family, they will not understand. These problems should, however, be considered so that anyone who is in the position of helping a widow is at least aware that the problems do exist.

Unless there is some training, people do not know what it is like to be a widow until they become one themselves. One may understand the process, the stages through which one passess, but we none of us know how we will behave until we are actually confronted by our own problems.

5

Emotions are not obedient and tidy things. As the widow proceeds towards the third stage of Grief Work, which is adjusting to life without the deceased, she is liable to go back to the first stage and to say, 'It seems incredible to be talking to you. Sometimes I still can't believe he's died!' However, she will do this less and less as she moves on.

By this stage, life has probably improved considerably for her. The widow is feeling better. Her sleeping pattern and her eating pattern have become more normal. She has found that she can cope with life quite well. She has survived dealing with alarming things such as the income tax inspector and the bank manager. Her financial situation is clearer. She may have had to move house and is now settled in her new home. She may have been able to stay in her old home and has made some routine improvements; perhaps she has had the kitchen painted or bought some new curtains for the bathroom. Life has moved on, and changes have taken place since her husband died. She takes these for granted; it has all happened so gently and naturally.

She is seeing her friends again, gently taking up the threads of her life. She is not doing anything very taxing. She does not want demands made upon her and feels she has not very much emotional elasticity, but her life is much more normal.

She has some new confidence. She has faced problems and can be quite proud of herself because she has coped so well. She finds that time has gone by and she has survived.

She has, for instance, learned how to put on an electric plug. (This may seem trivial but this was something that gave me one of my earliest feelings of triumph and is an achievement cited by practically all widows, which is an interesting sidelight on our society!)

She has considered problems her spinster friends have always had to face, and now she knows that she, too, can cope and she does not have to feel inadequate.

She has found a handyman to do all those small repair jobs her husband used to do; mending a shelf bracket, cleaning the gutters. Sadly, she now has to pay someone to do the chores her husband did on a Sunday afternoon – replacing a cracked window pane, renewing the rubber band on the vacuum cleaner – but this is the price of widowhood and she accepts this philosophically.

Then one morning her fragile house of confidence comes tumbling down. Her electricity bill arrives. She now understands the general shape of her budget and she is expecting it to be about £60.00. But imagine her horror when she reads the bill and finds it is for £6000.00!

We, of course, know – and part of her knows this, too – that it is a computer error… surely, it must be, mustn't it? But, as it stands, it is a legal debt. It is more money than she has in the world. She is panic stricken. Worst of all, she no longer has a husband sitting on the other side of the table with whom she can share the problem. There is no one to whom she can turn and say, 'Look, what the silly idiots have done this time!' – and by sharing the anxiety, feel better. She has no support and comforter when she is frightened, no one to restore her sense of proportion. And it it *she* who must now go to the Electricity Board, to confront them and sort the matter out. The Electricity Board is not the easiest of organisations to deal with as we all know. But she does go up to see them. And she is successful. She comes home with an amended bill. But something else has happened. She is different. She is tougher. She has changed, and she does not quite know herself. She is not entirely the same person her husband knew.

Whether she likes it or not, she is adjusting to life without her husband.

In this third stage of Grief Work, a widow will have to confront the problem of laughter. This may be a very strange statement, but just think about it...

Perhaps there has been a really funny programme on television which made her giggle to herself for the whole thirty minutes. Or she may have been on an outing arranged by some local organisation. Perhaps it was a trip to the seaside, and she has really enjoyed herself. When she came home, she suddenly felt very guilty and ashamed – although she would probably not admit this. But what is she thinking of – 'How could I be so heartless? To go off and laugh in the sunshine while *he* is lying dead in his grave?' What she has missed are the private jokes, the quick understanding which made for shared mirth and now it seems she has forgotten him so quickly?

What a dreadful wife she has been. What a dreadful person she now is.

Quite simply, she is feeling a very common emotion. She feels guilty to be alive, when he is dead. And she now finds she is still able to enjoy herself. Like many feelings, this appears totally irrational.

A widow, in the early tumult of grief, does not know on which feelings to rely and which is insubstantial. People do feel guilty and ashamed. These feelings are surprisingly common. However, although painful at the time, they do pass and heal.

Perhaps one of the things that helps in this healing is the recognition, however reluctantly given, that to her, as a person, her marriage was only an interlude in her life. She may not like it in the very least, but the fact is that she has more time to live. Whatever her age, whatever the length of the relationship, she is still a person in her own right, with a life of her own. She may not want a life of her own, even resent it bitterly, but it is a fact. She must do something with her life, because she has to live it each day, and hope to achieve something positive.

Perhaps she spent many years working to make a reasonably happy marriage, looking after another person. Now, suddenly, all her energies have been thrown into reverse. She has only herself to consider. She does not know what to do with these energies and feelings. Widowhood has been imposed on her, throwing all her previous life, routine and habits into chaos.

Is it any wonder that widows feel angry?

The last stage of grief work is known as 'Saying good-bye and reinvesting in life', and this is a very vague and misty area.

You do not forget someone you have loved. How could you, when you have spent thirty or forty years putting up with all their irritating little ways, enjoying the support and comfort they give; sharing the problems and the laughter? As you go on with your life, they are still part of you, still exerting their influence on how you have learned to feel and think. It would, really, be ridiculous to expect you could do anything other than remember.

Perhaps the best definition of this Task is when one can think of the dead person with sadness but without pain.

Our children are always our Achilles Heel. I think of a woman who had been to the wedding of a young cousin and told me: 'It was dreadful. I saw Sarah coming up the aisle, looking so beautiful, a real traditional bride in a cloud of white, on her father's arm, and I suddenly realised that if my Jenny ever marries, she doesn't have a father to give her away! It would have been his right and her expectation. If she does marry, we'll have to scratch round for some moth-eaten old cousin – and who'll make the speech for The Bride? I remember Tom used to say, 'Jen, you'll have to get married in a Registry Office, I can't make speeches. Do just elope, darling, it'd make life so much easier!' and Jenny teased him, 'If I did get married in a Registry Office, there'd still be the wedding breakfast after-wards. I couldn't be married without you and Mum there, I wouldn't feel properly married. You can't wriggle out of it, I won't let you, and anyway, you're the only person in the world who can make a really super speech, tell everyone all sorts of lovely things about me...' and he would laugh, 'Minx!' Jenny's mother was full of pain, she had tears in her eyes. Her feelings may have been a little exaggerated and out of proportion, but they were very real and I remembered that Tom had only been dead for about eighteen months.

A couple of years later, I met this woman in the local shop. She was bubbling over with delight. 'Isn't it marvellous! I'm so excited I must tell you. I want to shout it to the whole world.' Jenny had just telephoned from college, with her excellent graduation results. And her proud mother chattered on. 'You know, it was so sad Tom didn't live to know this, he was always so proud of her. But, there it is. He had to die some time, and there is never a right time, is there? If he was alive now but died next year, we'd have been saying, "What a pity he didn't live to see... to see her married, to see her babies." It would have been something else. At least he knew she had been accepted for college, he lived long enough to know she'd put her foot on that first rung of the ladder of her career...' There was still some sadness in her eyes, but she was smiling.

Long afterwards, she said to me one day, 'Do you remember when we met that day, when Jenny got her finals results? Well, the only sad thing was that there was no one in the world I could boast to, as of right, about Jen and how proud I was. I'm lucky. We've got a lot of friends, and they were all so pleased when I rang them up with the good news. But a child only has two parents. Tom was the only person I could really have talked to freely, who had the right to say "You sound like a proud parent", without it hurting... and it was sad he wasn't there, but it didn't hurt!'

❦ ❦ ❦ ❦ ❦ ❦ ❦ ❦ ❦ ❦

Why do we grieve? No one really knows. The scientists, psychiatrists and psychologists study this question of bereavement. They write books, make studies, publish papers on the subject. They consider questions of affective deprivation; bonding, mating and pairing. They wonder if the purpose of these activities is biological and to do with the continuation of the species. They observe animals: some species mate, produce the young and then part; others, like the swan, mate for life, and yet each species seems to continue perfectly satisfactorily. They propound theories about 'feeding' and 'protection' and the necessity of a male–female relationship in a group to prevent the males fighting among themselves.

No doubt these are all very interesting and worth-while topics, but perhaps they do not add very much to the reason why we grieve.

The reason why we grieve at 'the loss of a significant one' is, simply, because we love.

Grief is the price we pay for love. Perhaps many of these highly-qualified people ask the wrong question, and what they should consider is... Why do we love?

No one has ever been able to answer that question satisfactorily, but we all of us, scuttling about in the varied ant-hills of our lives, know we do this. We meet. We fall in love. We mate, we pair, we bond. We marry. We create a relationship with another person which very often lasts a life time, 'Until Death do us part'.

Perhaps we should turn from the clinical, scientific approach to this question, and for illumination, if not solution, we should consider another discipline, should look to the Arts. The Bible itself is studded with references, for example: 'Comfort them that mourn'. The list of quotations could be endless, but to confine to one or two... The old prophet wrote: 'Love is stronger than death' and he knew what he was talking about.

Shakespeare said, 'Who ever loved that loved not a first sight?' and a 17th century Frenchman had another insight: 'The heart has its Reason that Reason knows nothing of; Do you love by Reason?'

Love is not cool and rational. Bereavement and the ensuing grief is how we learn to cope with powerful emotions after the death of a significant loved one: what we do with overwhelming, free-wheeling feelings when the loved person is no longer there – and never will be again.

To help even just one other human being successfully come to terms with all the unexpected and highly complex problems which have suddenly confronted them makes Bereavement Counselling, far from being sad and depressing, a most deeply rewarding experience.

In counselling, both counsellor and client enter into another emotional relationship, gradually building up trust and profound intimacy. A good counsellor will monitor this process, will be aware when their client can exercise control and so go off, confident and happy, into the sunlight outside, and get on with their life.

Both parties involved in the successful completion of the Four Tasks of Mourning will then agree with Alfred, Lord Tennyson:

'It is better to have loved and lost

Than never to have loved at all.'